Eve

poems by

Betsy Orient Bernfeld

Finishing Line Press
Georgetown, Kentucky

Eve

for my daughter

Copyright © 2018 by Betsy Orient Bernfeld
ISBN 978-1-63534-511-7 First Edition
All rights reserved under International and Pan-American Copyright Conventions. No part of this book may be reproduced in any manner whatsoever without written permission from the publisher, except in the case of brief quotations embodied in critical articles and reviews.

ACKNOWLEDGMENTS

Grateful acknowledgment is made to the editors of the following publications where these poems first appeared:

"Bleeding in the Wilderness" in Western Press Books' *Manifest West – Women of the West*.
"Purple, Prickly" in *Third Wednesday*.

"Hiding in Plain Sight Close to Water" won Honorable Mention in the 2017 New Millennium Writings Literary Awards Competition.

An early version of "Rose Beth" appeared in the *Casper Star-Tribune Arts Section*. Portions are published here with permission of the *Casper Star-Tribune*.

Publisher: Leah Maines
Editor: Christen Kincaid
Cover Photo: Eve O. Bernfeld
Author Photo: Joe Bernfeld
Cover Design: Elizabeth Maines McCleavy

Printed in the USA on acid-free paper.
Order online: www.finishinglinepress.com
　　　　　also available on amazon.com

Author inquiries and mail orders:
Finishing Line Press
P. O. Box 1626
Georgetown, Kentucky 40324
U. S. A.

Table of Contents

An Alternative for Chief Justice John Marshall 1

White Flower 3

A Perfume Called Murder 4

Eve's Jungian Psychic Connection of Matter and Spirit Dream 5

If I Were Going to Build a House 7

Laying on Hands 8

Hiding in Plain Sight Close to Water 9

Bleeding in the Wilderness 12

Cathedral 15

Enchanted Lupine Forest 17

Raising the Mainsail 18

eve's post-freudian, feminist view of cigar smoking 21

The Red Room 22

The Flying Piano 25

Unnamed 28

Purple, Prickly 29

250,000 Miles to a Camellia 30

Rose Beth 32

An Alternative for Chief Justice John Marshall

Imagine a woman had sailed the Santa Maria.
Women are good sailors
in tune with the wind rolling
with the water swimming
sunburned ashore.

She would definitely have planted a flag
to prove to men that she had done it, discovered
not claiming for the pope but kissing
the earth whispering a prayer
to Maria.

She was so amazed by the trees
she picked and ate the fruit spoke
to the snakes and sipped
the crystal water dreaming
and dancing.

She was greeted by a man of bronze skin
plaited hair and exotic dress.
She met him eye to eye offering
her cherished blue glass
beads.

He said tell me your own words
that I may know you better.
She replied a heathen is one who worships the universal spirit.
A savage is one who yearns to ride horses.
A primitive furnishes her home with sky and mountains.
An infidel is one who breaks treaties.
I did not come to kill, conquer, slash, subdue, vanquish.
I came only to bleed.

Together they built an elaborate culture of beads and furs and feathers.
They traced their ancestry in stories not property deeds,
performed artwork every day, sang in court
and lived sacred.

In three rulings written from 1823-1832, U.S. Supreme Court Justice John Marshall set the basic framework of federal law concerning the legal status of Native Americans. Marshall, somewhat apologetically, justified the subordination of Native rights on the basis of the "actual state of things."

White Flower

Georgia O'Keeffe insisted
that her enlarged portrait of a flower,
despite the white fluted pelvis-like
petals and showy organs, was not
representative of female sexuality.
After all, the flower is androgynous.
She said she wanted people to notice
flowers, look at them more deeply,
and so she painted them huge.
The painting did catch my attention,
a whiff of dizzying desert perfume,
the silken corolla like white wings
circling slowly in the clockwise
breeze created by lilac and blue-green
shadows drawing me inevitably into the yellow,
pollen-stained center under delicate orange
anthers and onto the sticky brown velvet
cusp of the stigma. I sensed the discoloration
of my own birth and my present gaping
vulnerability. I fled backwards to view
the entire frame, the fragile, aching
beauty of Georgia's white flower.

Georgia O'Keeffe's painting "White Flower, 1929" is housed at the Cleveland Museum of Art.

A Perfume Called Murder

Why would someone
name a perfume so?
The color of amber
that ancient liquid
entrapped in the earth
for millennia.
I consider
as I gently
sensuously
trace my finger
along the outlines of the heart-shaped bottle
and test the aroma on my wrist slit my wrist
musky heavy like a bludgeon.
With the glass stopper I caress
my own heart-shaped body
on my neck for hanging
on my breasts for love
seeking the connection
horrifying
between love
and murder
and woman.

Eve's Jungian Psychic Connection
of Matter and Spirit Dream

It started out
as a rapid eye motion sleeping chase
dream someone after her.
She bought a ticket to San Francisco
she would get off in Tucson
she was on a train.
She woke up filled
with the realization cognition of time
out of sync if this were happening
now she would be on a plane
it must be 1955.
She slid back into the dream awake
deliberately unconscious continuing
to flee.
She left the train in Tucson
at her grandparents' house on Calle de Amistad she loved
that house sold after her grandfather's death.
Grandpa opened the door.
She said I am Eve a relative
Grandma and Grandpa showed her through the house
she knew every room so well
disembodied.
She saw the children Frances and Susan
her father five years old
but not clearly.
Grandma was warm and open
Grandpa was suspicious.
He cornered her in his den strewn
with papers and tools who
are you really?
If I told you
you wouldn't believe me
I will believe.

Your granddaughter from the future
Joseph's daughter.
Did Joseph become a doctor?
Remember vacations in Mexico
how you tell people you are a biology teacher
instead of a doctor?
She related the future of his daughters
his other grandchildren
how he taught her chess
made her chocolate sodas
watching operas late at night
she became more and more nervous
not wanting to tell him
he had died.

The images faded Eve
got out of bed. Outside
with her father on the front porch
her grandfather still
with her the air filled
with golden sparks
Aunt Susan and Cousin Sara
flying in today
for the family reunion
a butterfly in the dewy grass
dreaming.

If I Were Going to Build a House

I would not start with two stained glass windows
but it so happens that two stained glass windows
is what I have to start with. Windows
is not necessarily a bad start I mean
sunlight is already available
and what is the purpose of windows
but to stand between you and sky.

If I were going to build a house
I would not start with an oaken front door
sturdy and supportive as it might be
with a pre-installed doorbell even but a door
is what I have and night is already available
and what is the purpose of a door
but to stand as barrier between you and me
holding on by knob and hinge.

You laugh and say a house must start
with a foundation, a solid one at that,
and I say why? My stained glass windows
hold bunches of purple grapes and green leaves.
I'd say I have a regal start, a holy start. A house
is not just a foundation and a brick wall
but also doors and windows so that you can see
outside from inside so that you can get outside
from inside or inside from outside. At dawn
sunlight separates into slivers of gold and green.
At dusk my windows cast the purple light of wine.
You ring the bell and come in.

Laying on Hands

It was an unusual self-portrait
shot with her cell phone.
It wasn't her face. It was
her hand laid against the gnarled
trunk of an ancient maple, her hand
in soft focus, the tree trunk in vivid
detail, tense, wrinkled, splotched with red.
Are you holding your breath?

One could hardly make out
her close-clipped nails or the lines
of her knuckles or know that her fingers
in life were slightly curved at the joints
and in constant, balletic motion. Think
of a feather, she said, don't hold your breath
when touching, imagine blowing a feather.

Her long fingers were spread evenly,
each finger its own separate strength.
Are you tensing your shoulders,
gripping or grabbing as you touch?
Can the tree sense the ease
of her transfigured hand, her luminous
fingers, her breath whispering across
the hardened face like the flutter of a bird?

Hiding in Plain Sight Close to Water

I know a place hidden
within a patchwork of public
and private land little traveled
because it's behind a chained
but not locked fence
and because it is you see
so small but inside
this sanctuary is the river

> *the river was coming*
> *the Limpopo in flood*
> *following five weeks*
> *of heavy rain my husband*
> *ran with the children to shelter*
> *but my mother and I were slower*
> *my mother due to age myself*
> *due to advanced pregnancy*

several spring creeks and ponds
thickets of willows and a forest
of cottonwoods hunters have built
a duck blind in case I feel like hiding

> *there was no place to hide*
> *so close to water*

so far from the world
insignificantly tall
low to water but most of all

> *the torrent did not wait*
> *and Mother and I climbed a tree*
> *we weren't alone a dozen*
> *other people in our tree*
> *one a midwife for which*
> *I am very grateful*

I feel like sleeping in the open
meadow shielded from the road
by a tangled growth of
snowberries and wild roses

> *not a coconut not a cashew*
> *so there was nothing to eat*
> *nor milk to drink but soft*
> *leaves and prolific*
> *branches so we could lie*
> *in sturdy hardwood arms*

two mallard drakes take off
from a pond and four hens
float on the spring creek

> *for three days with the water*
> *only a few feet below dark*
> *and roaring*

as a major storm
is rolling in from Alaska
the plummeting barometer
singing bears to sleep

> *my mother gave up in the night*
> *hardly a splash but at dawn*
> *she was gone and then*
> *my labor started*

the moon huge and indistinct
behind a tissue of ice clouds
at a certain instant a point
of magic—just like the moment

> *the doctor dropped by rope*
> *from a jungle green helicopter*
> *cut the cord and took my baby*

before falling asleep when
your lumpy bed suddenly feels
so exquisitely comfortable
and you float weightlessly—

> *in and out of consciousness*
> *still no place to hide*
> *from cholera and malaria*
> *my beautiful child*
> *when waters subside*

the river turns to silver.

On March 2, 2000, Sofia Chubango gave birth to a daughter, Rositha Pedro, in a tree near her village of Chokwe, Mozambique as she clung for safety for three days above raging floodwaters.

Bleeding in the Wilderness

I've read that women should stay out of the wilderness
during their periods. It infuriates the bears.

Stepping into the woods
air thick with humidity
slurp of water, hint of breeze
not necessarily the sweet scent of flowers
but more basic, instinctual smells
leaves, pollen, mud.
I will never be a naturalist
recording the dates when each species blooms
let alone plucking a sample for the herbarium
or shooting a bird so it can become
a famous painting. The sight
of a wild rose is irrational, erotic.
Sniffing its center I am alive and once again,
bleeding.

During the thirteen hour ascent of Mt. Nez Perce,
off route, roped up, unable to release
the climbing harness to change a pad
and so bleeding down my legs
soaking through thick Air Force pants
all the way to the knees,
retching on the summit, regaining control
with measured breaths and small bits
of chocolate in my mouth,
rappelling down a waterfall
now wet also from outside in,
dragging home over blowdown trees
plastic bags of bloody garments.

Wandering three days from Rendezvous Peak to Hurricane Pass
sunburned, swollen, pounding headache,
studying high alpine flora, keying and classifying

in blinding light, never learning
one yellow composite from another
or identifying the penstemon,
peeing on miniature tundra flowers,
my knees like elephants, feeling the release
of the fertilized ovum and then plunging down
Avalanche Canyon pouring copious blood and tears
finally at Bradley Lake empty and thin
remembering only the forget-me-nots.

Walking carefully in the dark toward the Grand Teton,
sensing again the presence of small innocent company,
nibbling Underwood deviled ham on Wheat
Thins crackers, less nauseous as we passed
timberline and entered onto the rocks at 4 a.m.,
climbing guides ahead and above us
swinging their headlamps calling to clients,
edging past frightened tourists on Wall Street,
feeling at home on all the familiar pitches,
rejecting the free rappel on the descent,
instead hugging rough rock all the way down.

Laboring thirteen hours again
this time in the hospital a long wet birth
sucking chips of ice
taking in tiny increments of air
my stomach a mountain
each pain jagged
lasting three minutes hour
after bloody hour unable to speak
don't touch me
don't touch my bed swooping upward
toward a summit
walking off the gentler side.
My husband, the naturalist,
keeping time, writing notes for the doctor.

Under bright lights before anesthetic
delivering in rhythmic breaths
and wild uncontrolled bleeding.

The sun is coming up later now,
I am lazier, too.
The forest is full of goldenrod, fireweed, cone flowers
tall and solemn and most
ominous of all the purple fleabane.
Clouds of pine pollen are long settled,
today's haze is from Idaho fires
fertilization long over, flowers
coalescing to seeds
mellow bears plucking tiny huckleberries.

Cathedral

Immaculate Conception Cathedral in Kansas City, Missouri
was constructed in 1898, the same year
my grandmother was born in Wallace, Missouri.
The walls were astonishingly thick,
door jams a foot and a half deep. Her bones
were hard and thin, skin like yellowed
parchment stained purple with blood
from the IVs. This holy place.
I wonder how many times my grandmother
was here, head bowed in her Belgian lace
mantilla. The constant whoosh of oxygen.
The statues were lifelike and bloody,
St. Stephen stoned, the pews too short
for my knees. She was shrunken
under five feet tall, a white angel,
hands sculpted, each joint a round ball,
each digit slightly crooked from its neighbor.
Watching out the window, cars slowly circled
looking for a place to park. Someone abandoned
his car in the loading zone and dashed
for the hospital entrance. Golden tabernacle,
high airy ceiling, dark wood polished,
tiers of candles inside red glass flickering
with the prayers of the faithful.
One hundred years old. I want to die.
Why can't I die? Why won't you let me die?
Our Father who art in heaven, deliver us.
I filed her nails into perfect crescents,
buffing them until they shone.
Yellow orange sunset was blinding in the window.
Please, please let me die. Dark wood creaking,
thick velvet curtains on the confessional,
turquoise tube in her nose, brutally perfect breastbone
prominent on her chest, hands gnarled like a tree root.

"I am the root of all that," she said one Christmas Eve
as her children, grandchildren
and great grandchildren paraded past her,
"root" pronounced the Missouri way
like foot, Christ sitting waiting
in the cathedral.

Enchanted Lupine Forest

Take a walk with me, old lover,
down the river dike
into the enchanted lupine forest
infested with elves
and just starting to rain.
Meandering among the flowers
their colors tapering upwards
from dark to light, purple
at the ground then lilac
to lavender, cornflower
to sky blue, we can hardly breathe
for their sweetness.
Amid raindrops of perfume,
we hover under a mushroom
with the butterflies.
We could swoon for life.
We could marry again.
Now I understand
why purple shoes
are a perfect match
for a blue wedding dress.

Raising the Mainsail
for Jean Hahn

On a small sailboat in the Pacific just outside of Los Angeles Harbor, where monumental cranes painted purple, turquoise and red day and night load and unload the nation's trade with China, beyond the safety of the marina, past the lighthouse, it's almost evening and a long line of pelicans is heading for the breakwater, and we are the last sailboat out and the water has taken on an astounding royal blue. I am surrounded with lines and knots and vocabulary and physics complex as the sea itself, and I am determined to learn how to raise the mainsail, the most elementary and elemental task of sailing alone, not knowing that back home Jean had died.

    1. Pull the main halyard and two reefing lines out of the sheet bags and open their three stoppers on top of the cabin.
    2. From the side deck, open the shackle on the end of the main halyard that is fastened to the starboard stanchion and, after threading it through the lazy jacks, clip it onto the grommet at the top of the mainsail. Pull the slack out of the main halyard at the stopper.

I have written down the steps—all ten—in my journal and I keep studying them because it is so difficult for me to connect words with the immensity of pulling massive canvas into the wind. On the morning we set out for Catalina Island, the water had mellowed to a light blue, the mainland was draped in a thick marine layer, the wind barely moved us through the water. I had not heard the news but the sea turned to navy blue, then black with silver spray and we reefed the mainsail, moved the jib sheet blocks forward, and furled the jib to the second reef point. There was a period of unnerving uncertainty when the mainland coast disappeared into the fog and we could still not see Catalina Island ahead. Our hope was in our compass, a steady heading of 206 degrees. We stopped looking back and clung to the future, still in the mist.

3. Unwind the sail ties, boom vang and reefing lines, which are wrapped around the mainsail, and throw the boom vang line into the cockpit.

4. At the mast, pull the reefing lines forward, grabbing the outermost section of lines at the fairlead blocks, until the end figure eight knots are near the cabin-top stoppers.

5. From the cockpit, uncleat the topping lift, lower the boom a few inches, and re-cleat it at the second black mark on the topping lift line.

6. Uncleat the mainsheet and the boom vang.

We are sailing wing and wing off the south side of Catalina Island. The wind has finally come up this afternoon and is blowing hard. I learned later that Jean was eating lunch with two of her children at her favorite picnic spot at Moose right in front of the Grand Tetons, an early blanket of snow on top and in the foreground aspens bedecked in gold. Not really my mother, but my mother really. She simply fluttered away. Wing and wing is a tenuous point of sail. The pilot has to keep the arrow on the wind vane pointing straight back. Too far off and the mainsail could jibe, very dangerous at this speed. The roiling sea is making a straight course ever so difficult, but at the top of every wave there's a tiny lift when I feel I am flying with the grace of a bird. The clouds have thinned in random places and the sun is shining through all the holes.

7. Facing directly into the wind, pull the main halyard by hand and, as the sail rises, watch that it threads through the lazy jacks and no reefing lines get caught anywhere.

8. When the resistance gets too strong, close the main halyard stopper, wind three wraps around the winch, lock the line, and crank the mainsail the rest of the way up with the winch handle.

9. Remove the halyard from the winch and coil it into the sheet bag.

10. Cleat the boom vang line and the mainsheet.

I could see that October wind and rain had been at work during our absence, but the bleakness that greeted me at home was not the landscape. I had even missed the funeral. I headed to Jean's house up Skyline Hill with a carrot cake to visit her daughter. The aspen trees lining the road had kept their uppermost leaves, now even brighter gold than in September, like candles lit. It would take a few more windstorms and rainy days to put out those fires, but treasures of leaves lay like gold medallions on the ground waiting for snow and chickadees played among the white, barren branches.

eve's post-freudian, feminist view of cigar smoking

At the picnic table
among the cottonwoods
in the half moon
caressing phalluses
with punctilious gestures,
there was nothing the men had
that the women didn't.

In the mirror the next morning
the amber specks
in her blue eyes
fanned into yellow flames
and smoke still hung
like a gauzy scarf
around her hair.

The Red Room
>   *Pinedale, Wyoming*

The fireplace was so unnecessary
in the overheated room. The wallpaper
was red, the bathroom that same redness.
The quilt was old-fashioned patchwork,
scraps of fabric cut in flower shapes,
lots of reds. The dark hardwood floor
creaked so I walked the edges of the room
so as not to disturb my boss, the Judge,
in the master bedroom directly below.
There wouldn't be any such amenities in jail,
no red walls or flexible, forgiving floors,
just bars, cement and harsh lights,
for life.

Before dawn, the Judge and I,
the only guests, walked six blocks
to the courthouse in down jackets, mufflers,
wool hats, gloves and headlamps, the lighted
bed frame marking the bed and breakfast
still glowing on the front lawn. Snow plows
patrolled the streets, diesel pick-ups warmed
their engines heading to the rigs, the bitter
wind braced us for more bleeding photographs,
more damning testimony.

Lisa was 25 years old, beautiful and rich.
She came to Jackson Hole on a wild and free
adventure. On the road back home, her final trip,
she wore tan Patagonia stand-up shorts
like all the cool Jackson people
with a little cocaine in her pocket.
She had a pink wool sweater tied around her shoulders,
Ivy League even in the car, her hair curled
at six in the morning. Maybe her appearance
was what drove him to rage,
her left hand destroyed,
her long legs and white tennis shoes
splattered with blood.

In the steam-heated courtroom
the police recounted Lisa's every move.
She had played tennis the night before,
eaten dinner at the Calico then went hot-tubbing.
She slept at her best friend's house,
said good-bye at 5:30 a.m.,
picked up muffins at the Bunnery at 5:45
and stopped at the light near McDonald's at 5:50
next to a big Forest Service truck.
Who wouldn't have noticed her—
a blonde in a blue Jetta with a wind surfer on top?
She darted ahead of the Forest truck
before the road narrowed to a two-lane,
headlights still on in the dimness
of the early summer morning.

The defense presented a computer-generated aerial view
of the thirty-mile passage through Hoback Canyon,
showing every curve and turnout,
the fast-flowing Hoback River and the dark trees.
They plotted the progress of the Jetta from 5:50,
past the traffic light and into the canyon
followed by the Forest Service at a slower pace,
the vehicles depicted by the beam of headlights.
Surprisingly, three other cars had been on the road
that morning and remembered, their headlights
all on the computer.

Still, there was a three minute window
when the killer had slipped in and out
of the canyon unnoticed by witnesses.
He punched her in the face, shot twice
and was gone before the Forest Service men
came upon her body in the last turnout.
The man at the defense table
was white as a ghost.

Three minutes of untraceable time.
What if the Forest Service men had driven faster?
What if the muffins hadn't been out of the oven?
The defendant had worked the rigs outside of Daniel
and the other side of the party scene. Perhaps he provided
drugs and expected to get paid. What if he
had only shot once? What if the window
had only been two minutes, or one
minute, thirty seconds? What if I
awaited the verdict in a room that was cool
and blue?

The Flying Piano

This is the story of a daughter leaving home. It takes time.
The piano is a 1904 August Förster probably manufactured in Dresden.
Its history is lost until 1984 when Eve wanted piano lessons.
The old upright belonged to Kamla, who lived down the street
in a huge house with many rooms and goats out back.
Friendship between the two girls began when Eve was two
and Kamla five and I'd call the relationship foundational.
They invented the games Cat & Dog and Devil World (with goats)
and Eve was instructed in the concepts of Death and God.
When Kamla moved to Colorado, Eve got the piano.
We borrowed a dolly from Eve's music teacher.
Eve's Dad, his friends and several neighbors pitched in
to wheel the instrument down the street, someone drumming
Chopsticks, up our wooden sidewalk, around all the corners
into Eve's bedroom, a small town event I watched
from the window, opening the front door at the right time.
We had to get rid of Eve's bed.

The piano was scarred and the ivories stained,
the music holder hung unsupported on one side,
but lifting the top and peering down into the strings,
you could see it was an antique, polished and ornate.
The sound board was good, Eve's teacher declared,
and that's all that matters I guess.
Lessons lasted only three years, Eve hated practicing,
she refused to cut her fingernails, but the piano stayed on.
She displayed her dearest treasures on top—candles, tiny boxes
and earrings from her friends, a photo of her Dad's family,
her Dad about seventeen and cousin Rebecca a small child.
All those years, the best part of my life,
no one played the piano.

Eve left Wyoming at eighteen, still the piano stayed.
I dusted it, but never indulged my secret desire to play.
I'd call that a lost opportunity. My grandmother had a piano
and played by ear. My sister took piano lessons from a nun.

I listened to her practice. When she was finished,
I pored over her music books and figured out the easy songs.
I was terrified of piano lessons, instead I learned to type.
I taught myself at first and then took classes, my fingers
so fast I was sure I would have been great on a piano.
I saved a piece of Grandma's sheet music, rosy red cover,
eighty-five cents, Side by Side, ragged and funny,
what if the sky should fall?

Eve came home at twenty-eight and bought her own place.
She borrowed a dolly from the Pink Garter Theater,
her Dad, her friends, and a neighbor wheeled the piano
onto a motorcycle trailer, ate raspberries from the bushes
in our yard, and drove to the new house.
I cried as the piano went through her door,
a monumental moment of leaving. Eve didn't stay long.
Within three years she was back East in Chicago,
her renters in charge of the piano. Then she put the house
on the market and moved to Portland, Oregon
lock, stock and barrel, except for the piano.
I would have taken it back, but the old spot was usurped
by her Dad's new gun safe.

Eve arranged for a piano tuner in Driggs, Idaho
to store it in his shop. It needed all new strings.
He would haul it to Portland when she had space.
I was in charge of meeting the piano man at Eve's house,
empty except for the battered old instrument.
Upon his call, I raced over from work.
He had a marvelous delivery truck with a built-in winch
to pull the piano up into it. It was all very quick.
I stayed behind to pick up the few little bits of paper
that had accumulated underneath the piano
and smoothed out the carpet. Of course, I cried,
then I locked the door and the house sold.

In 2009, the piano still waits in a shop in Driggs,
but, really, it's hovering in the sky.
I see it in my dreams against a backdrop of turquoise,
the Grand Tetons are a tiny dark silhouette
across the bottom of the canvas, the half moon is above,
there are no clouds. It is supported by the power
of my typing fingers. They call that keyboarding now,
as if it comes anywhere near playing piano keys.
It is home and hope suspended, heavy as sorrow.
Soon Eve will call for the piano and it will be delivered.
She holds onto her piano just as I do.
Then my sky will be empty.

Unnamed

Eve said it was okay to hope.
She said it's no worse
when the worst happens
to have hoped for the best.
And so I allowed it. I let
the flower I had been clutching
tightly inside me start to open,
tentatively, its coral red
petals peeking from inside
tense sepals and breaking forth
in a bud. The second day
there was more, the beginnings
of a rose.

I wondered if I dared
to hope further. No sooner
thought than the taut
petals relaxed outward,
the many many more red
orange layers spreading forth like a riot
of petticoats, the aroma intoxicating. Still
I kept the rose hidden in my heart,
tucked away, and when I dared
to look again—in the middle of the night—
I saw another head spring up beside it.
It seemed safe in the dark
so I watched it, powder pink,
another rose, I was in the City of Roses.

I tried my best to hold back
but I admit to wild delight then
in one horrible moment, the roses
turned to straw. Yet here I am now
sitting in a field of wildflowers,
real ones, red, pink, yellow,
purple, blue, white, gold and
I am stunned with peace.

Purple, Prickly

The purple pricklypear cactus
more purple than ever this year
due to drought and cold
beautifies the canyon walls
on the steep trail to Elephant Head
the mountain I have loved
all my life still there
my life in prickly
segments now purpling
childhood home demolished
elementary school flattened
junior high slated for takedown
pink church going Father gone
my bloom yellow with red center
opening in the morning
closing in the evening
just once forever.

250,000 Miles to a Camellia

I have enough miles on my truck's odometer
to have driven ten times around the Earth's
circumference or one time to the moon.
And this is not my first truck. However,
most of my driving has been on Highway 22
to 89 to 80 to 40 to 15 to 28 to 70 to 89 again
to 40 again to 17 to 10, in other words from
Jackson Hole, Wyoming to Tucson, Arizona
to see my mother. Or on 22 to 31 to 26 to 20
to 84 to 5 in Portland, Oregon to see my daughter,
my Irish tea always in a metal thermos mug
studded with stars and moons and ethereal sea
creatures in the cupholder at my right hand. I still
haven't stopped at Mom's Café in Salina, Utah
where they advertise homemade pies and scones
on the side of their corner building. Where

I am standing now along my beaten path
I am gazing at a tree of flowers, leaves
deep waxy green, blossoms so like roses—
multi-petaled, layer after layer of fluffy
white tinged with pink, stand-up bright
yellow stamens, but no rose-like aroma,
no thorns—and I don't know what it is.
I have to ask its name. Perhaps I have not
traveled far enough yet. In all those miles

shouldn't I have gone somewhere more exotic?
Is it enough to always know where the moon is?
The simple plant from which my tea is steeped
came to me historically by clipper ship
semi-circling the globe in its own way
through the China Sea to the Indian Ocean
around the Cape of Good Hope, west of the Azores
to the English Channel. It did well in the Isles
as an ornamental, avid gardeners hybridizing,

expanding its family to hundreds of species,
intent on increasing the voluptuousness
of the petals, from a single cup to semi-double
to plethora, ignoring the nourishing value
of the leaves. Then it sailed back across the Atlantic
landing in America's Deep South where climate
felt more like home and it rose to the height
of fashion and eventually pushed onward,
carried by lovers to the Northwest, too cold
though wet, where flowers grow on trees.

Rose Beth

I saw the beads in the museum knew
they were mine
Prehistoric Paiute Artifacts.
I was a long time dying days
as slow as in childhood
my hands cracked always catching
pieces of hair and wool.
I lay awake bones aching watching
my hands watching
my pretty beads watching
the sand.
The sun made the sand shine warm
to touch I etched
a footprint in it taking days
to make it perfect pressed
my face into it.

   * * *

I am Beth.
When I was a child I wanted
to be Twig. Lovable Twig
wore nothing but a diaper her hair
in a topknot. As soon as I could
write I sat
at Mother's desk copied
the book about Twig.

When I was twelve I became
fat and began
to bleed. Dimples
in my legs large breasts I shut
myself in my room the entire summer threw
glitter jumped off the bed trying
to get to the Neverland.

I lost weight way
too much weight
my periods and a lot of my hair
so ugly.
The doctor told Mother I might
die. Mother began watching
out of the corners
of her eyes. She hugged me every day
to check for ounces gained
or lost.

I took up ballet. At Christmas
I danced the part of a Japanese doll
there were six of us Mother didn't know
which one was me. We wore
white paint on our faces black
hair piled on our heads kimonos
pillows. She stared
at each of us trying
to discover a characteristic motion.
She thought my hands
would give me away but they moved
too quickly with long curved red
nails weaving hypnotizing
patterns.

I got married. I wanted
to get out of the house but Daddy
built me a house like Mother's. I wanted
the bathroom fern green he painted
it white. I spotted
a mink's house at the top
of a neighbor's burn pile rescued
it from the flames I fancied
its simple wooden construction peaked

roof circular hole in the door I wished
it were my house. If only
it were larger or I as small
as a mink.

I got a job in a bakery
owned by a woman with thick black
hair enormous breasts using only natural
ingredients no preservatives no refined
sugar no shortening only
honey soybean oil every morning
turning out twenty-five trays
of sweet buns blueberry
walnut apple raisin peach pecan banana
cashew. I labeled
her goodies with drawings of mad
religious thorazine experiences onion
rolls with wings bagels in bow ties ladies
dressed in banana skins. I ate
nothing.

I took up running. Mother
doesn't know I do this. I keep
my Nikes in a box in the back
of my closet. Three miles five
miles ten miles not too far
for this battered body. I run
through sagebrush my head back a doe
sniffing the air. In the autumn
I hear the guns of hunters I keep running
not knowing if I too am shot sensing
confusion expecting
my strength to suddenly leave. I long
for the blue green sky
to fill my wide blank eyes.

Mother grew old. At first
I thought she was imitating me beginning
to hang onto the pews in church suddenly
afraid to open her birthday presents taking up
tap dancing. I have become
a collage of deaths the oboe teacher
shot by a burglar the old lady
drowned in the trailer court
swimming pool the neighbor boy's
motorcycle wreck my own
slashed bicycle tires. I remember
my own birth dark
tunnel bare feet drumming
drumming of Mother's heart.
I have been running starving
this same road for centuries my footprints
washing away in the wind.

I wanted a baby. Mother wanted
me to have a baby too. The doctor said
I couldn't have one but I gained
a few pounds became pregnant. In the whitest
part of winter in red
searing beauty I delivered
a daughter Rose Beth.

I am practically a skeleton. My hands
are crooked wedding ring
too large for my finger. My back
rounded I am conscious
of the glands in my neck.
I have no breasts no buttocks large
ankles. I am careful
not to bump myself on things so painful
even to sit at night I rest

by Rose's cradle on a padded rocker I stay
awake bones aching watching
my hands watching
my pretty baby listening
to my heartbeat.
There's no beginning no end
there's music
in my sallow blood.

      * * *

The archaeologist on his knees
opened the ancient wooden tomb the bones
of a woman nearly turned to dust but neatly
lined in row after row where
her chest would have been
part of a burial dress hundreds
of shining pearls.

www.ingramcontent.com/pod-product-compliance
Lightning Source LLC
LaVergne TN
LVHW041553070426
835507LV00011B/1071